A Color Guide to

PHOTOGRAPHY

Martin Hodder

CHARTWELL BOOKS INC.

ACKNOWLEDGEMENTS

Frank Blackwell, *pages 20 (photos below right) and 22 (photos above)*; Color Library International, *front cover inset (bottom) and pages 4, 5, 7, 18, 26, 35, 37, 38, 39, 42 (below), 43 (below), 46, 47, 55 and 59*; Martin Hodder, *pages 10, 14, 17, 19, 25, 27, 29, 45 (below), 50 and 60*; Japanese Cameras Limited, *page 9*; Olympus Optical Company (U.K.) Limited, *front cover inset (top) and page 8*; Barry Pickthall, *title page and pages 11, 15, 32, 33 and 40*; Picturepoint Limited, *front cover inset (center), back cover and pages 30/31*; Polaroid (U.K.) Limited, *pages 52 and 53*; Tony Stone Associates Limited, *front cover and pages 13, 23, 36, 41, 42 (above), 43 (above), 45 (above), 51, 56, 57 and 61*; Mike Wilson, *page 24*.

Illustrations by Sackville Design.

Designed and produced by

 Intercontinental Book Productions, Berkshire House, Queen Street, Maidenhead, Berkshire, SLF 1NF.

Printed in Hong Kong.

Contents

Why Take Photographs?

Photography is a leisure interest that everybody can enjoy. A camera can capture a fleeting moment in time by one click of the shutter. But to reach a level of expertise where the camera is always ready for that never-to-be-repeated shot, it is necessary to study the techniques quite thoroughly.

Unfortunately, most people under-use photography. An enormous number of households possess at least one camera; very often there are several cameras in each family unit. Yet, by and large, these cameras are used only two or three times each year.

Vacations are the peak time of camera use, followed by Thanksgiving, Christmas and New Year Eves, and then the occasional family outing. Birthdays and other family events may also spark off temporary interest in picture taking.

Yet there are so many other occasions on which we can use cameras. A photograph can recall an enormous variety of enjoyable events for years to come.

Photographs can be used to record all the important moments in our lives from birth to old age. A photographic record of the development of a family is, after all, the best record you'll ever have of this unique event.

In addition to vacations and anniversaries, which are so often photographed, all sorts of special events, journeys, celebrations and achievements can be captured with your camera. Even your work can make a photographic exercise. The people you meet and the places you see, the peaceful beauty of the countryside and the bustle of a modern city, can all be photographed, as can sporting events, circuses and parades.

Modern technology in the form of instant cameras, where all you need to do is to press the shutter release, can make photography a simple, almost foolproof pastime. So you should not need a special

People figure prominently in many photographs. Whether the photograph is of a beautiful young girl on a beach, as here, or a craggy-faced grandfather, a little care taken over composition and lighting will reward you many times over in the final result. Remember to keep the sun off the face, thereby avoiding hard shadows and ugly squinting. Here the exposure reading was taken by holding the camera close to the subject's face and then moving back to take the picture. A wide aperture (f/2.8) was used to throw the background out of focus, while a shutter speed of 1/500 sec retains detail in wind-blown hair.

reason for carrying a camera. And you can become as adventurous as you like.

Photography is very rewarding and it need only be as expensive as you care to make it. This book will, I hope, help to transform your snapshots into real photographs through a combination of advice, information and encouragement.
Note: The technical details given in the captions throughout the book are suggestions as to those most likely to achieve the given result. Depending on the conditions prevailing at the time, different settings might be needed.

This shot of the Arc de Triomphe in Paris is an example of good travel photography; note how the camera has been positioned to give a less common view of the famous structure, while the inclusion of the news-stand in the foreground adds color, atmosphere and scale. Bright conditions meant that a small aperture (f/11) could be used for maximum depth of field, together with a reasonably fast shutter speed (1/250 sec) to stop most of the movement from passing traffic and pedestrians.

Special events are a must for the photographer, while an action sport such as skiing can produce tremendous results. Ski pictures — like most sports — are best shot on color film. Use of a slow shutter speed (1/30 sec) together with very careful panning, keeps the subject sharp and the background blurred with an overall impression of speed.

Photography Grows Up

The idea of photography has been with us for a long time. The knowledge that images could be formed on a surface inside a darkened room – the *camera obscura* – is believed to have originated in ancient China, but it was many centuries before this theoretical knowledge could be put to any practical use.

First Principles

In A.D. 1000, the Arabian scholar Alhazen wrote that images could be formed by light passing through a tiny hole. Leonardo da Vinci wrote about the same phenomenon some 400 years later. Had da Vinci published his work when he wrote it, he would no doubt have been credited with the invention of the camera, at least in principle.

This honor has in fact been given to Battista Della Porta, who published a book on the *camera obscura* in 1558. His work may well have been based on da Vinci's findings.

Early Developments

The only refinement needed to create the camera itself was to utilize a lens instead of the pinhole. The first man to do this was a Frenchman, Nicephore Niepce. Some of the images he made between 1825 and 1827 are still in existence.

Louis Daguerre patented the world's first successful photographic process, announced in January 1839. Using silver iodide, he produced direct positive pictures on a metal plate.

William Henry Fox Talbot produced fixed negatives on paper as early as 1834, but this process needed much improvement. In September 1840 came the world's first reproducible photograph, and the beginning of photography as we know it.

From the days of Daguerre and Fox Talbot onwards interest in photography increased, and the techniques developed rapidly. By the 1860s it was part of the way of life of the wealthy, with the incredible popularity of the *carte de visite* and the drawing room stereoscope.

A print made from a negative produced in 1844 by William Henry Fox Talbot, the inventor of the negative-positive method of photography. It shows Fox Talbot's three daughters, posing for their father at their home. (*Photo. Science Museum, London.*)

Popular Photography

Photography for everyone came in 1888 when George Eastman introduced the Kodak No. 1. This was a box camera, measuring a little less than 17 cm (7 inches) by 10 cm (4 inches), with roll film sufficient for 100 exposures. When the film was finished the complete camera was mailed to Eastman's works in Rochester, New York, for processing and printing, and the camera came back reloaded.

Today, cameras have been to the moon and have played a vital role in space exploration. They are used for all forms of scientific, industrial and medical research.

They give pleasure to millions of people and a form of photography – television – plucks moving images, in living color, out of the atmosphere, for home entertainment all over the world.

Photographic research is continuing, yet it still relies, in principle, on the notes made a thousand years ago. The simple cartridge-load camera bears an uncanny resemblance to the very first Kodak in both specification and performance.

Technical developments will ensure that good picture taking becomes possible for everyone. Even the business of recording the photographic image will become electronic, with photographic film, as we know it now, gradually being replaced by electronically recorded images (as with video). Photography also plays a great part in the future development of mankind, as has been proven by both American and Russian space programs. This photograph was taken during a weightlessness training exercise while Gemini 4 was orbiting the earth. The camera was a Hasselblad, the standard issue for the entire American program.

Choosing Your Camera

There are many different types of camera available, and within each group there is a wide choice of individual models.

The Basis of Choice

Two important factors should influence your choice of camera – the type of photography the camera is likely to be used for, and the amount of cash you have available for its purchase.

The first consideration, the likely use of the camera, is important and can be broken down into three sections:

    (a)   Very simple snapshots, taken on vacations and special occasions.

    (b)   Simple photography over varying situations with a desire for really good picture quality.

    (c)   Varied photography needing good picture quality and wide versatility.

As a general guideline, cameras may be broken down into three corresponding categories, in ascending order of cost:

    (1)   Cartridge load and instant-picture cameras.

    (2)   Simple 35mm models of the 'compact' or 'rangefinder' type.

    (3)   Single lens reflex 35mm cameras and the larger-format rollfilm models.

Generally speaking, if your photographic requirements fall into category (a) you will find your needs satisfied by buying a camera in category (1), and so on.

The Simplest Cameras

Most of the first group of cameras are simple to use and nearly every model available will produce satisfactory pictures given reasonable conditions. Photographers who don't see themselves as anything other than snapshooters should look at cartridge load cameras first.

The least expensive *cartridge load cameras* have no control over exposure, and thus can only be used in good light, or with flash. As the price increases, so does

A typical SLR camera may seem to have a great many controls, but many models now offer automation if you want it.

A good 'compact' camera, while simpler and cheaper than the SLR, will well satisfy many needs.

versatility in the form of exposure and focusing control, together with lens quality. At the top end of the market the camera is highly versatile. However, if you are considering purchasing an expensive cartridge load model you would be well advised to consider a camera from categories (2) or (3).

Instant picture cameras fall only into the first category, and their prices vary enormously. They are excellent for instant snaps, but more expensive to run than conventional cameras.

Compact Cameras

Models falling into the second category, *simple 35mm cameras*, offer the simplicity of the snapshot type plus the advantage of the larger 35mm film format. All have automatic exposure control, permitting photography in conditions from quite nearly dark to bright sunlight, and nearly all have focus control.

They are referred to as 'compacts' and are good enough to satisfy most photographers in many situations. They usually

have a fastest shutter speed of 1/500 sec., enough for action photography, but they are difficult to use for close-ups and their lenses are not interchangeable.

Single Lens Reflex Cameras

Two factors, the wish to take close-ups and to use different lenses, are the overriding reasons for choosing a single lens reflex camera (category 3). The S.L.R. is, without doubt, the camera for the serious photographer. It offers extreme versatility, very accurate exposure metering and is easy to operate. For this reason it is more expensive than the simpler models.

Being able to fit wide-angle or telephoto lenses is a great attraction, widely extending the scope of your photography. With an S.L.R. you view through the lens and therefore see precisely what will appear on film. Metering, also, is through the lens, guaranteeing accuracy. Many models now have automatic exposure control, making the S.L.R. simple to use and capable of producing really professional results, even for the amateur photographer.

9

Lenses and Accessories

These three pictures show the difference that various focal lengths can make to a scene even when photographed from the same viewpoint. The first picture shows the use of a 24mm lens on a 35mm camera, giving an impression of spaciousness. The second picture was taken with a standard lens, which is roughly equal to the view seen by the eye. In the third picture a 200mm telephoto lens has been used, bringing the far point of the pier sharply into view.

People will often spend a long time choosing a camera, then rush out and buy their additional lenses with only a moment's thought. Another common mistake is to buy an expensive camera and fit it out with cheap lenses.

Choosing a Lens

Bear in mind that the quality of the image recorded on film is decided primarily by the optical quality of the lens fitted to the camera. The most commonly bought accessory lens is a 135mm telephoto. Yet, strangely enough, the photographer who cares about his work is more likely to benefit from the purchase of a 24mm or 28mm wide angle lens.

When considering the purchase of a lens, think carefully about your photographic interests. If action, sport and candid photography appeal to you, then you need a telephoto. But, if you favor 'pictorialism', landscapes and town views, a wide angle should come first.

Whatever type of lens you decide on, choose it with care. For sporting and action enthusiasts, a 200mm lens will be more useful than a 135mm, but it will be more expensive. Even more versatile will be a zoom. At one time zoom lenses lacked optical performance, but now they can be used with confidence.

Virtually all telephotos are good, but this is not true of all wide angles.

With all lenses, buy the best you can afford, but with the shorter focal lengths (particularly below about 25mm) it is especially important to avoid buying the cheapest.

The Basic Kit

The most useful outfit for the person with a 50mm or 55mm standard lens who is still

Sometimes a scene needs the addition of something really special. Although the fish-eye lens is often over-used, there are occasions when they can be beneficial. They can be highly expensive — $4000 and more for certain cameras — but some of the independent lens companies produce them for much less. Cheaper even than fish-eye lenses are fish-eye effect filters which fix onto the front of an ordinary lens. This shot shows the type of effect which can be achieved by using this kind of attachment on an 80mm lens. The exposure was f/8 at 1/250 sec.

experimenting would be a 200mm tele-photo (or an 80mm to 210mm zoom), and a 24mm wide angle.

Camera Accessories

There is a wide choice of photographic accessories but only a few are necessary for everyday photography:

Flashgun
No photographer should be without flash; medium to high-power electronic units are most useful.

Lens Hood
This helps keep direct sunlight off the lens, thereby reducing glare, and protects it from rain.

Exposure Meter
You will need an exposure meter, too, if your camera does not have one built in. They are compact enough to carry around with the rest of your equipment, and convert the light measurement into a series of shutter speeds and f-stops.

If you're quick it is possible to get action pictures which look like this. The trick is to fit a zoom lens, and quickly alter the zoom setting during exposure. It's a technique which requires practise; aim to shoot on a dull day, which permits longish exposure times, and to set the shutter to give a half or one-second exposure. Set the camera on the tripod, mounted firmly, and then operate the zoom control as you trip the shutter.

Tripod
A tripod is essential for longer exposures and night-time photography. Use it with a cable release to prevent any camera shake during long exposures.

Filters
Always fit a haze, ultra-violet or skylight filter when using color film, since it will give better haze penetration, bluer skies, more sky detail and crisper, brighter colors. When using black and white film, a yellow or orange filter provides a good general image contrast and gives much better sky detail, with more pronounced clouds. Cross-screen filters, which may be fixed over other filters, provide star-burst effects from reflections and other sources of light. All filters protect the lens.

Choosing a Lens

Type of photography	Suitable lenses
Dramatically over-emphasized wide views with extreme distortion	Fish-eye
Wide views with or without deliberate distortion	10mm-20mm
Wide views with dramatic impact; tall buildings; confined spaces; narrow streets	20mm-35mm
Landscapes, views, street scenes, general work	35mm-65mm
Portraiture, glamor	55mm-100mm
Candids, athletics, tennis	100mm-200mm
Football, cycling, motor sport	150mm-500mm
Golf, ships at sea	250mm-1000mm

Today's photographer has more opportunity to achieve special effects with filters than ever before. The great popularity of the single lens reflex camera has done much to popularize the use of filters; SLR models enable the user to see the precise effect through the viewfinder and, in the case of colored filters, through-the-lens metering takes the light absorption properties of colored filters fully into account.

Our photographs here show a number of points. In picture one, an ultra-violet filter has been used, in hazy conditions, to cut through some of the haze and thereby provide more clarity all round. The second photograph shows the effect of adding an orange filter to the same scene — giving a warm, sunset-type glow, to the picture. Picture three demonstrates the use of soft-focus filter with a clear central spot. The camera was carefully lined up so that the clear central area was pointing straight at the ship's funnel — producing an extremely pleasing, rather unusual, overall effect. When using filters of this type, be certain to use a small aperture (about f/8) in order to make use of the clear central spot. Using a wide aperture (say f/2.8) would produce an overall soft effect, which is precisely what this sort of filter is designed to avoid.

Filters for a Purpose

Filter	Effect on Color Film	Effect on monochrome film
Haze	Haze penetration	Haze penetration
Ultra-violet	Haze penetration	Haze penetration; darkens sky
Yellow	Yellow cast	Haze penetration; darkens sky; improves cloud detail slightly.
Orange	Orange cast	Good haze penetration; darkens sky noticeably; much better cloud detail; darken greens; lightens oranges and reds.
Red	Red cast	Good haze penetration; very dark sky with extreme cloud detail; increases overall contrast; darkens blues and greens; lightens oranges and reds.
Polarizing	Reduces reflections from glass, water, china, etc, but not metal. Strongly emphasizes blue skies without affecting the overall color balance of the photograph.	

On some occasions extra impact can be added by the use of special filters – known, in fact, as effect filters. Here the photographer has brought extra life to a photograph of a customized car by using a filter which picks up reflections of sunlight and breaks them up into star points. These filters are commonly called star burst or cross screen filters. In this particular case the filter is so designed as to further break up the reflected beams of white light into the colors of the spectrum. Exposure on a bright day, with slow color film, was f/11 at 1/125 sec.

Sunsets make great pictures – but sometimes the overall color of the scene isn't warm enough to convey as much atmosphere as it could. The answer in such a case is to use a yellow or orange filter to provide the yellow-orange feeling of a romantic sunset. Here the photographer has used a yellow filter with an exposure of f/8 at 1/125 sec, to achieve a colorful effect.

Getting the Most from Your Camera

A camera is a tool for taking photographs and, like all tools, it should be made to work for you so that you can create the best possible photograph from the raw material of the scene before you.

Many cameras possess a number of controls which can be used for more than simply getting a sharp, properly exposed picture.

The Choice of Aperture

The most useful control is the aperture ring. It controls the amount of light passing through the lens into the camera's interior. The size of the hole governs the area of sharpness recorded on film.

Imagine you are photographing a line of fence posts stretching away from beside you to the horizon and passing across the viewfinder in a near-diagonal line. Your focus is set at 15ft (5m), meaning that a post at that distance is perfectly sharp.

With an aperture setting of f/2.8, only that post and the area 2ft or 3ft (1m) in front and behind it will be sharp.

Now reduce the aperture to f/16. With that simple move all the posts from 7ft (about 2m) away from you, to the horizon, will be sharp.

This area of sharpness is called *depth of field* and it is a vital consideration for every photograph taken.

Distance from subject and *focal length* also influence depth of field. Except for very close focusing, depth of field extends two-thirds behind and one-third in front of the object being focused on, and increases with distance. And, given the same aperture and distance from subject, a telephoto lens will provide less depth of field than a wide-angle lens.

The Value of Large Apertures

For portraits, pictures of single flowers, and for any other isolated subject, it is usually best to have the minimum depth of field. Always select a large aperture for this type of photograph – not less than f/4 or, perhaps, f/5.6 with a standard lens. Thus, with the camera focused carefully on the subject, the background will be recorded only as a meaningless blur, forming a useful 'backdrop' for the subject to stand against.

The same method can also achieve those abstract splashes of color which are sometimes seen in the foreground of outdoor pictures. With the camera focused well past them, bunches of brightly-colored flowers near you are transformed into a colorful blur which can provide a pleasing, soft surround.

When to Use a Small Aperture

Most landscape pictures look best when everything is in focus, from the garden in the foreground to the mountains on the horizon. Here you need an aperture of f/11 or f/16, the latter giving an enormous depth of field.

Seeing the Depth of Field

With most single lens reflex cameras the effect of different aperture settings can be seen through the viewfinder. If you have a 'stopped down' or 'closed aperture' metering camera the differences are apparent as the aperture is adjusted for metering. With 'open aperture' cameras there is usually a depth of field preview button which, when depressed, closes the aperture down to that selected, thus permitting you to see what's happening. Checking the effects of different aperture settings is a habit well worth getting into.

Here we can see the effect on depth of field of shooting the same scene with first, a large aperture and then a small setting. At f/1.8 only the railings are sharp, with the building becoming very soft. At f/16 practically everything is sharp, from a couple of feet from the lens to the far background.

Choosing the Right Shutter Speed

The second creative control of any camera is the shutter speed, which is especially useful when you are photographing a moving subject.

Many people imagine that the best way to do this is to use a fast shutter speed. A good test of this belief is to photograph passing cars; take shots at speeds from 1/500 sec to 1/8 sec, carefully panning the camera as the cars pass you.

Study the results afterwards and see which picture best conveys the feeling of movement. You will probably choose that taken with the slowest speed. Not all photographs of moving objects should be taken at very slow shutter speeds but your selection can have a profound effect on this type of picture.

Photographs like this are perhaps the best way of portraying the atmosphere of a city center at night. The only way to capture the traces of car lights is to use a long exposure time – here it was probably 20 seconds. An aperture setting of f/11 gives a suitable exposure and plenty of depth of field.

Choosing the Exposure

The following is intended as a guide to exposure in some of the more usual photographic conditions and can be used when operating without an exposure meter. The aperture settings quoted are based on a shutter speed setting of 1/125 sec.

	50ASA film	100ASA film
Bright sunlight	f/8-f/11	f/11-f/16
Hazy sun	f/8	f/11
Sunny, but in shade	f/4-f/5.6	f/5.6-f/8
Cloudy	f/4	f/5.6
Heavy overcast/rain	f/2.8	f/4

These figures assume photography

These two photographs show the effect of using a fast shutter speed, and then a slow one on a car moving at 40 mph. The fast speed (1/500 sec) stops all movement in the car and the background. The camera was panned with the subject during exposure, but the result is a picture completely without a sense of movement. For the second picture a speed of 1/8 sec was used. Again, the camera was panned but here both the car and the background are blurred, with an exaggerated sense of movement.

from mid-morning to mid- or late-afternoon in summer conditions. During the winter each set of conditions will require an exposure increase which might be as much as one f stop. However, when photographing in snow the figures in the tables can be used without modification.

Focusing – Depth of Field

Every camera employs a system of focusing to give a sharp image to the subject being photographed. But, depending on the distance to the subject, the area of sharpness (depth of field) will alter: it extends roughly one-third in front of and two-thirds behind the subject, and increases as the lens is focused for distant subjects. Maximum depth of field is obtained by focusing at the *hyperfocal point* – the nearest point of sharpness to the camera when focused at infinity. If you focus at infinity, two-thirds of the depth of field ('behind' infinity) will be wasted. If you refocus at the hyperfocal point, the depth of field will extend from a point halfway between this point and the camera to infinity.

Simple cameras often have fixed focus settings for portrait, group and landscape pictures.

The rangefinder system of focusing uses two images, obtained from two windows. The picture is in focus when both images coincide.

Some SLR cameras use a split screen focusing system. Here, the picture is in focus when the lines across the center join and the fresnel ring is seen to become clear.

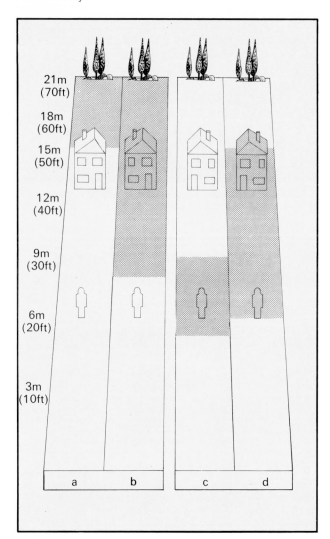

a   b   c   d

The photographs above show the different effects on depth of field of focusing (left) at infinity and (right) at the hyperfocal point. The foreground detail is much sharper in the latter photograph, although the background retains an equal sharpness.

Depth of field: (a) When focused at infinity, two-thirds of the depth of field is wasted. (b) Focused at 50 feet – the hyperfocal point – the depth of field increases by half the distance from this point to the camera. (c) Focused at 20 feet, the depth of field is shallow. (d) Focused at 30 feet, depth of field is sufficient to render both major subjects sharp.

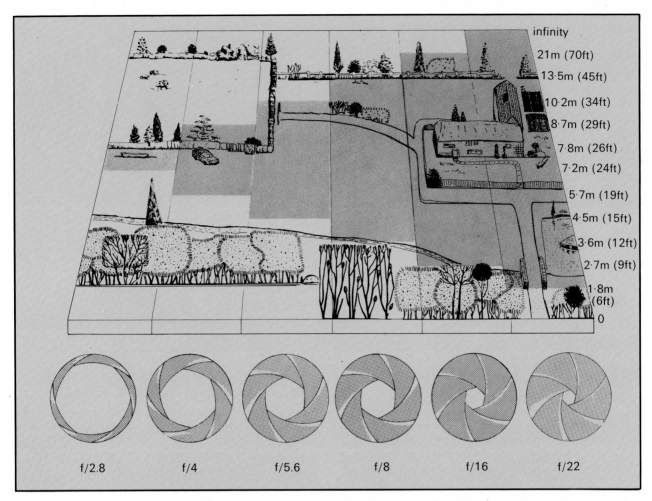

infinity
21m (70ft)
13·5m (45ft)
10·2m (34ft)
8·7m (29ft)
7·8m (26ft)
7·2m (24ft)
5·7m (19ft)
4·5m (15ft)
3·6m (12ft)
2·7m (9ft)
1·8m (6ft)
0

f/2.8   f/4   f/5.6   f/8   f/16   f/22

Aperture – Depth of Field

The size of aperture – and thus the amount of light entering the lens – is expressed in terms of f stop numbers. These are calculated by dividing the diameter of the aperture into the focal length of the lens; for example, an aperture 5mm in diameter on an 80mm lens would be expressed as f/16, an aperture 20mm in diameter as f/4, and so on. This constant relationship between aperture and focal length means that all lenses set at the same f number should admit the same amount of light.

The size of aperture also affects depth of field. A small aperture will result in a much greater depth of field than a large aperture. Since focusing also affects depth of field, theoretically the greatest depth of field possible will be obtained by setting the aperture at f/22 and focusing on the hyperfocal point.

Changing the aperture setting affects the depth of field. Given the same focal length and focusing distance, a large aperture such as f/2.8 will obtain a much smaller area of sharpness than a small aperture such as f/22.

Focusing on the rose in the center of the picture, the aperture was changed from f/16 (left) to f/2 (right). The larger aperture (right) results in a shallow depth of field; the central rose is still sharp, but the foreground rose and the church in the background are out of focus.

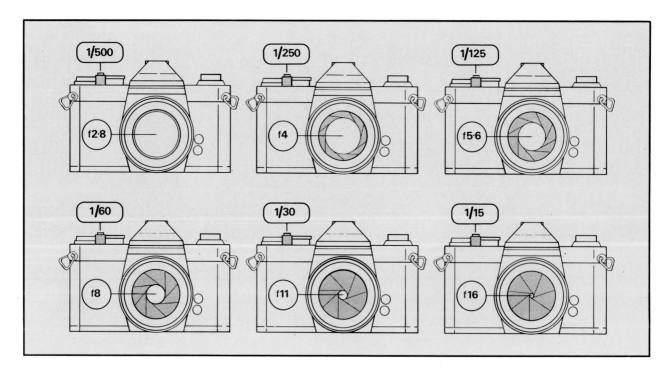

Combining Aperture and Shutter

Various combinations of shutter speed and aperture settings can be used to vary the image while retaining the same exposure.

The aperture and shutter speed controls follow a similar series, and have a similar effect upon *exposure* – the amount of light entering the lens and acting upon the film. Decreasing the aperture by one stop (f/2.8–f/4) halves the area of aperture and therefore halves the exposure. Similarly, most shutter speed settings are marked in fractions of a second in the progression 1, 1/2, 1/4, 1/8, 1/15, 1/30, 1/60, 1/125, 1/250, 1/500. Each new setting is about twice as fast as the previous one, and this also halves the exposure.

If exposure is to remain constant, any change in aperture must be matched by a compensating change in shutter speed, and vice versa. Under normal lighting conditions, you can choose from several combinations of the two controls for any one exposure, and so achieve different effects of depth of field and/or speed when photographing the same scene.

In the photograph below left, the aperture was set at f/2.8 and the speed at 1/250 to freeze the action. In the central photograph, the speed was dropped to 1/25 but the aperture remained at f/2.8, resulting in overexposure. In the photograph on the right, the speed was again 1/25 but the aperture was decreased to f/8 and the camera panned to blur the background and give an impression of speed.

A wide aperture (f/2.8) reduces the depth of field, making the subject stand out clearly against a softened foreground and background. A shutter speed of 1/500 sec stops movement, and backlighting provides highlights on the dog's coat.

Lighting to Advantage

Most outdoor photography is done under straightforward lighting situations – the sunlight is kept behind the photographer, often coming from over one shoulder.

For most pictures this provides the best contrast in tones and the most effective rendering of colors.

With inexpensive cameras it is in fact unwise to attempt photography in any other lighting situation. Cheap lenses cannot cope with too much light falling on them and direct sunlight on the lens will cause severe degradation of the image.

With any camera it is normally a mistake to shoot with the sun coming from directly behind the photographer. The result can appear 'flat' and people in the picture will not be able to avoid squinting. It is better to have the light from the side, which provides more detail and overall improvement in image quality.

Back Lighting

If the camera can cope with it, sunlight behind the subject is very effective in certain cases. The sun can shine through a person's hair and some form of reflector (even a sheet of newspaper will do) can be used to throw light back on the face for extra detail.

Photographs involving trees and foliage also work well when backlit, and a high proportion of successful landscapes have the sun shining toward the camera.

Any photographs of water will be better with the sun coming toward you, and light reflecting from the surface, throwing up reflections from wavecrests.

Remember that lighting can frequently be controlled and it pays not to accept a lighting situation as it is first seen. Move around and explore the potential of different picture angles.

Composing Better Pictures

It is easy to undervalue the importance of composition. A little thought about the way pictures are put together will make all the difference to their quality. Even if you only use a camera on vacation, care over composition will give you much better pictures.

The Main Focal Point

The first area for consideration is the main focal point of the picture. When you are sure of this, then all other aspects can be arranged so as to throw emphasis on the area of prime interest, and so produce a good effect.

Let's imagine that your family is paying a visit to the countryside and you want a picture of the children. Far too many people simply stand the youngsters up, tell them to smile at the camera ... and it's done.

If the family is visiting an interesting place, then why not photograph not only

A simple picture of a pleasant rustic scene. The atmosphere is conveyed to the viewer as much by the way the photograph has been composed as by the scene itself. If a picture jars on the eye, it is hard to take in instantly, and probably won't achieve its purpose. If a photograph is pleasantly composed, however, it will always be a joy to look at. Composition even comes into simple scenes, and in this particular example takes the form of the position and angle of the old cart. Note how it occupies the lower left-hand one-third of the shot, (most good pictures can be broken into thirds, both across and up) and that the angle of the cart forms a near-diagonal line. Exposure was f/11 at 1/60 sec.

Composition is all about photographing something in such a way as to provide a picture which has the most appeal, or impact, or which depicts the subject in the way you want to see it. These three pictures of a motorway bridge give an idea of what can be achieved with a mundane subject. The first is an overall view; the second shows it photographed from an ordinary viewpoint with a standard lens. In the third photograph a 24mm wide-angle lens was fitted, and the bridge was photographed from a close, narrow-angle viewpoint. A small aperture (f/16) has given maximum depth of field.

the children but also some interesting aspect of the surroundings? The main point of the picture can be the youngsters and behind them, or to one side of them, can be a recognizable part of the scenery. That way you get a picture of the kids which is interesting and more meaningful.

Don't overdo it though, and have distracting foregrounds or backgrounds. *Don't* have trees and posts protruding from heads, and if you position people to one side of the picture make sure that they look toward the center of the shot – not out of it.

Framing Your Subject

Pictures often work well if the main subject is somehow framed, perhaps by trees, foliage, doorways, windowframes, bridge arches and so on. A photo of a local view is usually more effective with someone in the lower left or right-hand corner looking into the scene. And what about using the line of a stream, or a road, or a hedge or fence, to lead the eye in to the main point? Mentally breaking the picture into thirds, both vertically and horizontally, and then arranging the components within these areas, makes pictures more effective. Country views for example, which are one or two-thirds sky, look better than those where the sky slashes a line straight through the center.

The Right Camera Position

Always consider the position and direction of the camera in relation to the subject.

Don't assume that the best position is with the camera held at eye-level. If the people you are photographing happen to be shorter than you are, you may foreshorten them, for example. Pictures which include water often look better with the camera held down, near the water. It is well worth experimenting to find the best angle for different types of subject.

Light and Shade

Watch out for shadows which intrude into the picture, and shadows which perhaps benefit it. Note the effect of the sunlight from different angles – see how it can shine through the hair, giving wonderful highlights, or how it can bring water to life by sparkling as it reflects from the surface ripples.

As you become aware of composition you instinctively start to construct the pictures better. It's then that you stop being a snapshooter and become a photographer.

Color Photography

Everything we see is in color and consequently, there can be no disputing the fact that color photographs are more realistic and more lifelike than are black and white pictures. For this reason, color photography is understandably the most popular form of the art.

A color film is an unbelievably complex material, and today's emulsions are the result of constant research and product development. Because of this, it is possible to capture colors which are tremendously likelike – so it is worth making the most of the color you see around you, and doing all you can to eliminate the variables which can be caused by inaccurate exposure.

Here's a really colorful scene which has been helped by having the strongest color (red) close to the camera. It was shot with the camera in a low position, using an aperture of f/16 for all-over sharpness.

Colors are best recorded when lighting conditions are bright. Because of the various processes involved, the camera can only record an image which, in terms of color, is slightly sub-standard to the one we see. Compare the colors of the countryside on a dull, rainy day with the same scene on a bright, sunny day. When colors look dull and subdued to the eye, they will be even less colorful when photographed.

Colors are always brighter when the sun is reflecting from them. So for all normal scenes, views over water and pictures of people, the most colorful photographs will come when the sun is behind, or at least to one side of, the photographer.

However, there are exceptions. Some subjects are at their most colorful when light is being transmitted through them.

Color Slides

When using color reversal film (for slides) any under-exposure will result in a darker transparency. If you're photographing something and you particularly want to emphasize the color, try deliberately under-exposing by a half or one f stop. The colors will be stronger, more saturated.

When photographing sunsets you can in fact cheat by under-exposing (if using reversal film) and thereby heightening the colors. Another trick at such times is to fit a yellow or orange filter to make the colors even stronger.

Color Prints

When using color negative film, make every effort to ensure correct exposure in all circumstances. Good prints, with truthful colors, will only be obtained with a properly exposed negative.

Tobago, in the West Indies, was the exotic setting for this sunset. The scene was rather colorless, unusual for the time and place, so an orange filter was used to give the expected warm glow of sunset. Exposure for this scene was increased by two stops over the indicated setting to provide the foreground detail which otherwise would have been recorded in silhouette. Settings, for high speed color film, were 1/60 sec at f/4.

With careful camera positioning it was possible to shoot this mountain view with the small red house adding a splash of bright color to a scene otherwise devoid of it. Mountain views are always dominated by greens and blues, and a splash of red inevitably helps pictures like this. With a 28mm lens, 50 ASA film was exposed for 1/30 sec at f/11.

How Filters Can Help

The use of haze, ultra-violet and skylight filters will aid color rendition by producing a picture which is crisper overall. The only way that filters can actually enhance colors is to use a polarizing filter; this aligns the rays of light reaching the lens in such a way as to provide the best-possible color rendition, mainly in the sky, although other colors might appear brighter too. However, don't expect a polarizing filter to help except in bright sunlight.

Color Films

There are two types of color film – *reversal* (for color slides), and *negative* (for color prints). Either may be developed by the user in some cases, but some color films of both types can only be handled by professional processing laboratories.

Home processing of color films is not difficult, but it is not an area suitable for the beginner. Experience with black-and-white processing is recommended before starting on color.

Fortunately there is no difficulty in commercial processing. The quality is extremely high, and processing by commercial specialists can be less expensive than doing it yourself. Only experience can tell you where to find the best combination of price and quality, and advice from friends may be helpful when you start.

Make Sure Your Film is Fresh

When buying a color negative film, check the expiry date printed on the pack. This is the last date on which the manufacturers consider the quality of the emulsion can be relied upon to produce the best possible photographs. If this expiry date has already been reached or if it is only a few days away, ask for another film.

Color film should not be left in the camera too long. It should not be loaded in sunlight, nor should you leave the camera lying in the sun while it contains film. Remember that film deteriorates quickly in heat.

The latent image on the film begins to deteriorate soon after the exposure has been made. Therefore, aim to complete each film in a reasonably short period of time, and then get it processed as quickly as possible. In a hot climate film should be processed within a few weeks of exposure. One of the most popular times for taking photographs is when you are on vacation. If you want to avoid disappointment, par-

ticularly if you have been to a hot and sunny spot, try to keep the camera in the shade and get the films developed quickly on your return.

Getting Prints Made

Color negative films may be processed by mail order companies, or by the local camera shop or the neighborhood chemist or drug store. It is always advisable to check prices first.

There is probably little to choose between processors in quality. One advantage of using local shops is that the results can be checked on the spot; if you're not satisfied there should be no. problem in rejecting the prints.

It is best to ask for small prints. Then, if you wish, selective enlargements may be made at a later date.

If prints come back with an overall color cast, this may be the fault of the processing company, in which case you should demand that they be reprinted. However, check the negatives first; if they are very dense, or extremely pale (indicating over- or under-exposure) it may be impossible to produce satisfactory prints.

Prints or Transparencies?

Color reversal film is more straightforward and cheaper. However, while a film show can be great fun, transparencies are less simple to view, and need to be projected for optimum enjoyment.

Many reversal films are bought 'process-paid', meaning that you pay for processing along with the purchase of the film. After exposure it is mailed off in the bag provided in the film pack, and you receive, in return, the processed, mounted transparencies. Excellent color prints may be made from these at little cost.

These three pictures show the effects, on transparency film, of under-exposure, correct exposure and over-exposure. Exposure was correctly calculated by simply pointing the camera into the scene, but angled down very slightly compared with the final result; this was done to avoid the meter being over influenced by the light reflected from the water and the ship's white superstructure. The center picture shows the result with the correct exposure of f/11 at 1/60 sec. The other two pictures show the difference made by just one f/stop either way of this. Note how the transparency exposed at f/16 (under-exposed) is slightly too dark, while the one exposed at f/8 (over-exposed) is too pale. The opposite effect occurs with negative films.

Better Techniques

The ability to study one's photography critically is the hallmark of an enthusiastic photographer. Only by being self-critical, by showing a willingness to listen to the comments of others, by being prepared to learn from other people and by learning from one's own mistakes can one become a good photographer.

Every roll of film exposed should be looked at critically. Mistakes should be noted so they can be avoided in the future, while minor discrepancies in exposure and composition can be rectified later on. By carefully studying every picture you take you can learn from your mistakes, and you can often improve the pictures you have already taken.

Check the exposure

The best way to check that mistakes are not being made in exposure is to use transparency film, even if your photography is done usually on negative film. Slides should be projected at a medium distance on to a screen and examined for exposure error.

If any are a bit dark, with over-emphasized colors, they have been under-exposed. Try to work out how you arrived at the exposure settings at the time and you might realize there was something about the situation which fooled either you or the camera. Slides which look washed out have been over-exposed, and with these too you should try to work out why this happened.

Improve the Composition

Now study each picture for composition. Is it an effective photograph, with impact and a clearly defined focal point? Or is it a jumble, without any sense of direction or main point of attraction? If any of your shots

fall into the second category, try to work out what's wrong, what's out of place, whether the lighting was from the wrong direction, whether the camera was held too high or too low, and so on,

The most effective photographs are always fairly simple without an over-abundance of components crying out for attention.

This peaceful scene benefits from having a different emphasis placed upon the main subject of the photograph by careful cropping. The reeds in the foreground are used as a soft frame for the figures in the boat, and the line of hills behind seems more dominating and powerful. A very long exposure of 10 seconds at f/11 was necessary in the low light.

No matter how careful one is over their initial composition, many pictures can be improved by cropping – cutting off certain areas in order to draw attention to the main point of the picture, and eliminating unnecessary features.

With slides this can be done by masking off with tape, but it is not a very satisfactory way because the picture left is inclined to be rather small. However, with

30

prints it is a different story, particularly if you make your own.

In the darkroom, the best way to crop is by viewing the projected image of the negative on the baseboard of the enlarger, covering different areas of it in turn to find out what makes the best picture. Then you simply print what you want by using the masking frame.

The second way to crop a picture is to cut off extraneous areas. Try it with some of your prints; several could probably be improved by careful cropping.

Ask the Critics

Other people's views are important, so try to find someone to show selections of your work to. If you get no reaction, something's gone wrong. Make a note of the pictures which receive appreciative comments. Shots which create an immediate reaction must have something going for them; work out what it is, and decide whether this ingredient could be included in more of your work.

Black and White Photography

Although the usage of monochrome film constitutes only a tiny proportion of the world's total, most of it is consumed by enthusiastic amateurs and, of course, by newspaper photographers.

Black and white photography is in fact held by most of the acknowledged photographic leaders to be the most expressive of all the photographic media.

When Black and White is Best

The choice between monochrome and color depends very much on the type of photography to be done. Photographs of the family on the beach, for example, are much better if taken in color. But a dramatic landscape or a picture of an industrial complex silhouetted against the late-afternoon light in mid-winter will be more effective when portrayed in black and white.

To make the most of monochrome film, you need to think even more carefully about what you are attempting to say with your pictures than is the case with color. Black and white does not lend itself to snapshot photography (despite the fact that it is much cheaper than color film).

Because of the types of subject for which it is suitable and the great care that is taken to capitalize on its advantages, it is not surprising that often the most truly impressive photographs are produced in monochrome.

Using Filters to Good Effect

When taking outdoor scenes you can get most impact from the sky by showing it as a medium gray tone, with clearly-defined clouds. Do this by using a yellow, orange or red filter. Yellow is probably the best for most pictures, while the red will give strongly emphasized sky and cloud definition.

Orange and red filters generally boost contrast in outdoor pictures, so for really dramatic, over-contrasty views, you can use a red filter.

Black and white film may also be assisted by using a green filter when photographing scenes which include a lot of green foliage which is important to the picture. The filter will lighten the green, making it stand out better.

The Right Film for the Job

One useful aspect of monochrome film is that it has much more exposure latitude

It is not by accident that most died-in-the-wool photographic enthusiasts do much of their photography in black and white. It is felt by many to be the most expressive medium in photography, despite the inroads that color has made into the hobby over recent years. This photograph shows why some people cling to black and white; for sheer photographic strength it would take a lot of beating, and it is difficult to imagine it being any better in color. Another advantage is that so much can be done to improve the end result at the printing stage. For this shot an aperture of f/8 was used at 1/250 sec and the whole scene was deliberately over-exposed to produce the silhouette effect.

Here we see the difference between black and white and color for the same photograph. While the color shot shows everything in full detail, the black and white picture takes on something of an abstract nature producing a more creative pattern effect in the timbers of the ship. Both were taken with an exposure of f/16 at 1/250 sec.

than color film. This has two benefits: good prints can be made from seemingly hopelessly over- or under-exposed negatives; and there's much more chance of capturing detail in areas of intense highlight or very deep shadow.

Black and white film comes with a wide range of light sensitivity (measured as an ASA factor, or rating). At the lower end of the scale is 25ASA film, suitable for really serious landscape work and capable of very large blow-ups. At the top end is 400ASA, providing exposure capability in all lighting situations. Recent improve-

ments to 400ASA film types mean that it can be enlarged much more than was at one time the case, and this type of film is universally popular with press photographers. We will examine these differences in speed more closely overleaf.

Better Prints in Black and White

Nearly all monochrome film is of the negative type; only a few enthusiasts using monochrome reversal films from which black and white slides are made.

Within the range of negative black and white film produced, there are, broadly speaking, three main sensitivity bands – slow, medium and fast.

The chemical structure of the film – the part which actually forms the image – causes the formation of grain in the developed film. On big enlargements this resembles grains of sugar or salt, and it is the type, structure and size of the grain which determines the sharpness of the picture.

Grain is governed by the way in which the film is made and developed, and by the film's sensitivity to light (the faster the film, the more pronounced will be the grain structure). Slow-speed films (those with a low ASA number) have the finest, sharpest grain structure, while high-speed films have more pronounced grain.

Choosing the Right Film

Most usual in the *slow-speed* section are 25 and 50ASA films. They are used only by professionals and those amateur enthusiasts who want to make use of the unique characteristics of this type of film.

Slow speed black and white film produces a sharpness of resolution and definition not to be found in other films. For photographs demanding the ultimate in sharpness, and for pictures calling for unusually extensive enlargement, this is the type of film to use.

In the center of the film sensitivity band come the *medium-speed* films. One of them, with an ASA rating of 125, is one of the most widely used by amateur black and white enthusiasts. This type of film combines fine grain characteristics with great capacity for enlargement.

At the top end of the sensitivity spectrum come the *high-speed* 400ASA films. These films possess the greatest exposure latitude (being most forgiving in exposure errors), have good low-light capability, yet still permit considerable enlargement. These high-speed films are becoming increasingly popular and are on the way towards replacing medium-speed films.

The image contrast in any given situation is also governed by the film's light sensitivity. If all other variables are eliminated, low speed films will always give noticeably greater contrast than high speed films. You will have to take great care to get the exposure exactly right, but the results can be superb.

The Film in Your Camera

The manufacturer's stated ASA number need only be used as a guide. For example, 125ASA film is often used at 200ASA, while 400ASA is used at anything from 600ASA to 1600ASA or even 3200ASA. Provided that development is adjusted accordingly, the film will be correctly exposed, although some image deterioration can be expected. Increasing the effective speed of your film in this way can be useful when your film is too slow for the lighting conditions.

Processing Your Own Film

Black and white film is simple to process at home, and you thereby have absolute control over your work.

For film processing you need only a developing tank, a thermometer, a measuring flask, some developer and fixer. For printing you also need an enlarger, print dishes and some print developer. This basic equipment can be bought relatively cheaply, secondhand if need be. The techniques of processing and printing are discussed on page 62.

Black and white provides the everyday photographer with a great deal of scope for exceeding the normal bounds of the pastime. Here's a superb example where a once straightforward portrait has been transformed into a combination of art and photography. The original print was retouched with well-planned and beautifully executed artwork, and then rephotographed to provide the final, artistic print. Both the technique and the technicalities are incredibly simple and can be mastered by anyone who has ever made a black and white print — although the final result depends on the individual artistic ability of the person in the darkroom.

Finding a Subject

Deciding what to photograph is one of the greatest problems with which most photographers find themselves faced. Yet after the first couple of films, some people think that they have already done it all.

Most people use a camera to record special events, with vacations, family anniversaries, celebrations and special outings right at the top of the subject list.

However, camera usage should not stop short with those ideas. The difference between the snapshot photographer and the enthusiast is, simply, enthusiasm. The really keen photographer uses his camera for all the obvious subjects, but goes out of his way to record all kinds of other events, in addition to photographing absolutely anything which he feels might make a good picture.

Extending Your View

Subject choice is not really limited by the type of camera one happens to have. Naturally, with a cheaper cartridge load model you will not be able to photograph motor racing, yachts far out at sea, or tiny insects crawling around blades of grass. For all those there is a need for specialist equipment.

Inexpensive cameras, without the facility for alternative lenses and, perhaps, without exposure control, will impose limitations on the way you photograph many subjects – but most can still be photographed.

Many people, for instance, take dramatic photographs of high buildings, with the camera held close against the structure, pointing almost straight up. It makes little difference whether the camera is an expensive single lens reflex or a cheap pocket model – you'll still get a similar picture. Naturally, image quality will be better with the more expensive camera, but the owner of a pocket model will still

obtain an impressive shot for the album.

Don't be deterred from photographing something which appeals, by the fact that you have only a cheap camera or because you don't rate yourself as a good photographer.

Discovering Pictures

Everyone with a camera should try to get into the habit of actually looking out for things to photograph, instead of using it only on the obvious occasions. Look around you, and think about the things which are there, waiting to be photographed; everyday objects like the bark of a tree, the bricks of a house wall, the reflection in a car mirror, the sun shining through the sails of a yacht drawn up on the beach, smoke curling skywards from a chimney, the sun shining through a clump of trees. The possibilities are endless.

Because of their symmetry and sheer impressive nature, many modern buildings make ideal subjects, and by clever use of the camera they can make fascinating pictures. This example taken in San Francisco, shows what can be achieved with architectural subjects, however simple their outline. A wide-angle lens adds to the impression of size, while standing close to the building and tilting the camera upwards gives a pyramid-like effect of converging verticals. Use a small aperture, of say f/16 to provide maximum all-over sharpness and a shutter speed of 1/60 sec.

Whether you want to take a portrait photograph, to enliven a vacation snap of a building, or to convey an atmosphere or mood, people make some of the best photographic subjects. This portrait of an old man provides evidence of the truth of this, conveying much of the character and experience of a grand old individual. Although flash was clearly used for this shot, the flashgun was held to one side, providing directional lighting which emphasizes the rugged old face, without being unduly harsh. A suitable exposure for this sort of photograph would be 1/60 sec at f/8.

Shape, Pattern and Texture

It's no coincidence that some of the most popular subjects for photographic club competitions are those for shape, pattern and texture. They are things which are around us all the time, but we are inclined to take them for granted. Attempting to photograph shape, pattern and texture induces constructive, creative thinking.

Shape can be seen, and photographed, in anything from a vase to an aircraft. The outline of a beautiful girl, seen in silhouette against the sky, forms a lovely shape – so, too, do the pebbles on a beach, or the wheels of a car.

Pattern is less obvious to many people, but exists everywhere just the same. Look how the sun shining through a long line of fence posts forms a pattern in the ground, or how a spiral staircase forms a rising pattern as it heads upwards. Look at the patterns on a freshly-plowed field, and see how they take on more or less emphasis with different positions of the sun. Still out in the country, look at a field of young wheat which has just been sprayed with weed-killer – note the patterns formed as the tractor wheels have compressed long, thin lines of wheat into the ground. Find a river with lots of twists and curves in it; get into the right position and these same twists might form an attractive pattern.

Texture is more apparent, but still passes unnoticed by most people. Some texture is easy to see. Some is more apparent with the light shining obliquely over it; while other textures only show clearly when the light is shining through something – like the veins in a leaf or the delicate structure of the petals of a flower.

Recording What You See

In most cases there is nothing difficult about photographing any of these things, although many photographers believe that these subjects are only for the user of black and white film.

Shape and pattern can be recorded in most cases by the simplest of cameras; the important component, in fact, is not the camera but the ability of the photographer to recognize a potential subject.

Texture sometimes requires more skill and a camera which will focus close to the subject and/or take close-up accessories. But the first and most important part is still to see the pictorial potential of what is before you. Success in photographing shape, pattern and texture indicates that not only have you mastered the use of your camera, but you are also well on the way to becoming an all-seeing, creative photographer.

Patterns are all too often neglected by the photographer. This shot of a skier has been well planned; taking the picture with the sun low and to one side emphasizes all the lines in the snow, which would hardly show with front lighting. Despite the brightness of the snow, a wide aperture, say f/4, would have to be used to give a reasonably fast shutter speed of 1/125 sec in the fading light, and with slow film.

In complete contrast to the lines a skier makes in the snow, the structure of this pier shows up much better with the sun shining through it into the camera. This angle means that the patterns of the structure complement the reflections in the water to make an interesting and pleasing pattern picture. With an aperture of f/5.6, a shutter speed of 1/250 sec would be necessary.

People, Vacations and Places

We all like to take pictures of the places we visit, and of our families and friends enjoying themselves. But with a little thought you can take much better pictures than the average snapshot.

Taking People as They Really Are

The best photographic subjects of all are people. There are not many rules about photographing people; in fact, perhaps there is only one – always photograph them in such a way as to depict their character, and the mood of the situation they are in at the time.

Really, it's very simple. People relaxing on a picnic should be made to appear as though they are relaxing; people enjoying themselves at a horse race meeting should look as though they are enjoying themselves; someone engrossed in their

hobby must actually look engrossed . . . and so on.

The secret of it all is that people should not be posed for pictures. Pure 'candids' are obviously the best way to do it, but for candid work your subjects must genuinely be unaware that they are being photographed. This normally means using a telephoto lens and shooting from a distance, or fitting a wide-angle lens so that because the camera is not actually facing them people may not realize they are being photographed. But don't be put off if your equipment doesn't run to these attachments; you can still take good photographs of people.

When people must be made aware they are to be photographed, I feel the best approach is to say: 'I'd like to get a picture of you, but please carry on with what you're doing'. Usually they will co-operate and the result should be a good picture of someone who doesn't appear to have been posed for the occasion.

Make the Most of Your Vacations

Vacations provide marvellous opportunities for experimenting with new subjects. Usually the photographer is seeing new places, people and situations and is in a totally relaxed environment.

Fishermen can always be relied upon to provide interesting vacation pictures, absolutely loaded with atmosphere. Fishing boats, and their gear, are always colorful, providing even more interest than many other scenes. Although this shot was obviously taken in late afternoon, the Greek sunlight was still bright enough to require an exposure of f/16 at 1/125 sec.

Paris is, traditionally, the most romantic of all cities. Here, the combination of the River Seine, the Eiffel Tower, sunset and warm evening light aids the mood. A magenta filter has produced the overall pink effect in the sky. A likely exposure in the low-light conditions would be 1/2 sec at f/11.

Take shots of people on the beach, enjoying drinks at outdoor cafés and (with flash) making the most of the night-life. Also photograph the environment, the local people, the trees and flowers, the shops, the markets, the street scenes, the airport and so on.

Airport Security Checks

One aspect of holiday travel which can affect photographers adversely is the X-ray equipment used during airport security checks. Because X-rays ruin film, it is advisable to adopt the following procedure.

Don't pack cameras and films in your main luggage, but carry them in your hand baggage. Tell the security officials you are carrying film, but don't worry if they still insist on putting it through a scanning

The mist playing round the mountains in the background, surrounding this snowy view of a fairy-tale Bavarian castle adds the air of mystery. A small aperture (f/11) would achieve this sharpness from foreground to infinity, necessitating use of a tripod for a slow shutter speed of 1/15 sec.

Local people going about their everyday business always make good vacation shots. For this market-day picture in Portugal the photographer stayed around long enough for the locals to become accustomed to his camera – consequently, no-one is looking self-consciously at it. A suitable exposure to get the best from this bright, front-lit scene would be f/11 at 1/60 sec.

machine. Many of these machines do not damage film no matter what other people might tell you. But if the equipment at the airport is not 'film safe', the officials will be happy to check you through by hand.

Town and Country Views

Anyone with an interest in the countryside and new places enjoys photographing views in towns and country.

For photographs around town, a wide angle lens is best, but don't worry if you have not got one, concentrate instead on detail.

Out in the country you'll normally need a standard or wide angle lens. The best shots come with the sun to one side of the photographer and, in the summer months, not later than about 10 a.m. or between 2 and 5 p.m. This is because the overhead light around midday tends to flatten detail.

Taking a photograph at just the right moment can produce something which is just a little different to the thousands of other shots of the same, popular subject. This picture of the Sydney Opera House was taken at sunset, but before the sun had disappeared completely. Using a very long exposure of about 10 seconds brings up detail in shadowy areas in these conditions: while a picture could be obtained using more conventional exposure times, a lot of details would be missing.

Reflections can play an important part in much of our outdoor photography. Here the picture was deliberately taken in still conditions. The smooth water at Fort William, Scotland, therefore, has produced interesting reflections which further add to an already interesting scene. Finding the right exposure in situations like this is a balance-operation; requiring detail in the dark background hills and the brightness of the white building. A good setting would be 1/30 sec at f/11.

Animals and Action

There are many types of animal photography but in the western world most people practice on domestic pets such as dogs, cats and budgerigars. From there, it is not too difficult to progress to zoos and safari parks, and even full-blooded safari work on location in East Africa, should you be lucky enough to go there. But don't give up just because you have to stay at home; it is still quite possible to take interesting and delightful animal pictures.

Pet Pictures

Pets are not easy to photograph because they tend to get up and walk away the moment they're faced with a camera, even if they have been posing perfectly for a couple of hours beforehand! So the two main requirements are a knowledge of your particular pet's habits . . . and a great deal of patience.

Domestic pets make really appealing subjects for photographs. Even so they should always be photographed when they are at their best and most photogenic. Most cats and dogs have playful moments, and this is really the time to picture them; try not to use flash because it could well frighten them off after the first exposure.

Wild Life Photography

Apart from the animals in zoos and safari parks, there is a great variety of wildlife to be photographed in most countries, and birds are especially interesting subjects. You need a telephoto lens for bird photography, but it is not really difficult – again, patience is a virtue. The best place to practise bird photography is near the coast, where seagulls spend hours soaring in the winds, particularly near cliffs.

Remember when photographing birds that they must not be disturbed during the breeding season, so keep away from nests. Even the slightest interference could lead to the death of the fledglings or failure of the eggs.

Action Photography

Many people steer away from action photography because they feel it needs outstanding skills and expensive equipment. This is not the case, although experience is valuable, and versatile cameras and lenses do provide you with more scope.

Sporting events provide most subjects for the action photographer, with everything from athletics to motor cycle racing to test your skills. For the newcomer, it makes sense to start with the slower-moving sports (like athletics), especially if your camera has only a limited range of shutter speeds and you don't have a telephoto lens.

Naturally, the faster-moving the sport, the more difficult it becomes to photograph it, especially with motor racing where you will need a range of shutter speeds, with a fastest of at least 1/500 sec, and a couple of telephoto lenses (or a zoom which has a maximum focal length of around 200mm).

However, all forms of sport offer lots of scope for experiment. Most pictures of motor racing show the car, which might be travelling at well over 120 mph, sharp in every detail. Try using a slow shutter speed, panning the camera with the car as it passes; with a bit of luck you'll get a picture containing background blur and the car sharp which simply cries out 'action'.

Action photography is not restricted to sport. Cars in the street, people walking, riding bikes and riding horses – they are all good subjects in their own right, and provide the action enthusiast with a chance to show his expertise.

Pictures like this require a lot of planning – they simply do not come by accident. In this case the photographer has sat in the back of the boat, and waited until the sun was shining towards the camera, and through the wall of spray. A medium telephoto lens was used with a very fast shutter speed to freeze all movement, including the spray. The aperture setting was f/8, providing a depth of field which was just about right for the situation. In any pictures taken from a fast-moving boat, such as this, the slowest shutter speed which should be used is 1/500 sec, because of the effects of vibration.

Animals can sometimes be used to add some atmosphere to a picture, and – if you're lucky – some foreground interest as well. In this case a third quality has been introduced by the inclusion of these ducks in a sleepy English village – an idea of scale. A 35mm lens was used, and the camera was held close to the ground. The aperture control was set at f/16 for maximum depth of field, with the camera on auto.

Daylight Photography

Taking photographs in daylight is the most natural way to use a camera, yet it is not without its problems. The good photographer controls the light to suit his work, and will avoid working in certain daylight conditions.

Choosing the Light Angle

The simplest way to control daylight is to photograph the subject from the direction which provides the best possible natural lighting effect. Nothing should ever be

Few people give due consideration to the direction of light when taking photographs out of doors. If they do, it's often to make sure it is coming directly from behind the photographer, square on to the subject. Usually, this is the worst way to use daylight! For many situations, the best angle of light is from one side of the subject; this photograph is a perfect example, with the sunlight coming from the right hand side at just less than right angles to the photographer. The result is plenty of light on the building (the Colosseum in Rome) but a sufficiently oblique angle to show up the detail, which would be lost with head-on lighting. An exposure of f/8 would give plenty of depth of field, with a time of 1/250 sec.

photographed outdoors without first thinking about the way in which it is illuminated, and then working out the optimum camera-subject-sun relationship.

Buildings, for example, are at their worst when photographed with the sun shining full on their front. This has a flattening effect. Far better to take the picture when the sun is coming more from one side, showing up any detail in the stonework or brickwork through the shadows formed by the directional light.

Landscapes are much the same, and are usually at their worst when the sun is directly behind the photographer. The same scene a few hours later, with the sun to one side, will be far more interesting. Some landscapes do not work well with the sun behind them, facing the photographer. The chief exception is when there is water in the scene, and the sun's position throws reflections into the camera.

There are two sun positions to avoid when photographing people. If the sun is directly overhead, and is bright, it could throw such deep shadows over their eyes that your subjects will look eyeless and quite terrifying. Also, try to avoid taking pictures of people looking into the sun; they will almost certainly squint and will appear to be featureless because of the flattening effect of direct sunlight.

Help Yourself to Light

The best way to photograph people is with the sun behind them, and with light reflected into their faces from a white sheet or piece of newspaper.

Because setting up a white reflector is not always possible, you can compromise by having the sunlight coming from a point midway between the camera and the subject.

Many people enjoy photographing flowers, and the translucent nature of most flower petals cries out for backlighting, so photograph them with the sunlight coming

from behind the flower. In this case it is simple to provide some frontal illumination; even a small piece of white card, or a handkerchief, held in front of the flower will reflect sufficient sunlight back on to it to provide adequate detail.

Dawn and Dusk

Note the way the color of the light alters shortly after daybreak and just before sunset. At the end of the day the light changes from white, through yellow to orange, and this will alter the color of almost anything photographed at sunset. So if you want to avoid whitewashed cottages looking orange, or a white shirt looking yellow, don't take pictures at this

Lighting which comes directly towards the camera can also be extremely effective. This is especially true when photographing views which include water, flowers and foliage. In the case of water, this lighting arrangement provides a brightness which would otherwise be lacking. Camera position is important too, for overall effect. For this photograph the camera would be held close to the water, using a wide-angle lens to provide a feeling of space. The smallest possible aperture, f/22, would provide sharpness from the center rock, only a few inches from the camera, all the way to the horizon. The camera would need to be tripod mounted for a shutter speed of 1/15 sec.

time. However, if the idea is to capture the atmosphere of sunset or sunrise, then you can enhance the color by fitting a yellow or orange filter to your camera.

Flash and Low Light Photography

Modern technology has made flash photography far simpler, and consequently more foolproof, than would have been thought possible only a few years ago.

Many photographers are introduced to flash work through the cubes which clip into cartridge load cameras. These cubes consist of four bulbs, each of which will provide the correct illumination for the average flash picture.

Automated Flash Photography

Automation comes into flash photography, either through automatic flash guns, or automatic adjustment of the camera's aperture when the focus is adjusted, or a combination of the two.

The need for adjustment (and consequently for automation) is because light loss increases with increasing flash-to-subject distance. To provide the correct exposure the camera aperture must be opened up for this greater distance. Shutter speed however, is not adjusted since the duration of the electronic flash is always less than the shutter speed. Thus altering the shutter makes no difference to exposure. In fact, each camera has a maximum speed at which the shutter must be set when electronic flash is used; this is not because of exposure considerations, but a requirement of flash synchronization.

Automatic flash guns have a light sensor which tells the equipment when sufficient light has been given for a picture and then cuts the light source. With the camera set at the aperture recommended with the flashgun instructions, and the correct film speed set on the gun, correct exposure is assured.

Some cameras incorporate a device which, when a flashgun is fitted to the hot-shoe on top of the camera, links the focus and aperture controls. As the focus is adjusted, the correct aperture is set to provide the right exposure at any given camera (and flash)-to-subject distance.

One drawback with electronic flash is that the light is very direct, tending to provide a stark image of people's faces. This is fine for use at parties, but not for serious portraiture.

The Use of Bounce Flash

The way round this is to diffuse the flashgun's light, either by reflecting the light from a convenient wall or ceiling (which should be white) or from a special umbrella reflector. This is a white umbrella and the flashgun is fired into its center; it then reflects and diffuses the light falling back onto the subject.

If a flashgun is automatic, with a reversible head, it may be used on the auto setting in this way. Otherwise, it must be used manually, and the exposure calculated by measuring the distance from flashgun-to-reflector-to-subject and dividing it into the guide number of the flashgun. To calculate the aperture, add one to two f stops to your answer to allow for the diffusion of light. To work out the aperture required without a diffuser, divide the flash-to-subject distance into the guide number.

Success without Flash

In low light situations without a flashgun a lengthy exposure time will be the only way to achieve a correctly exposed picture. Measure exposure in the usual way, then focus with care because the inevitable use of a very wide lens aperture results in loss of depth of field.

The camera should be mounted on a tripod or other firm support, and a cable release used to fire the shutter. If a cable release is not available, use the camera's delay timer, an equally efficient method of obtaining a movement-free exposure.

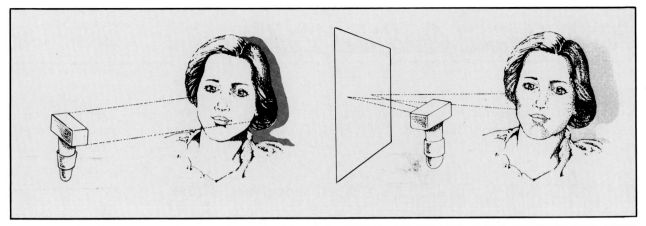

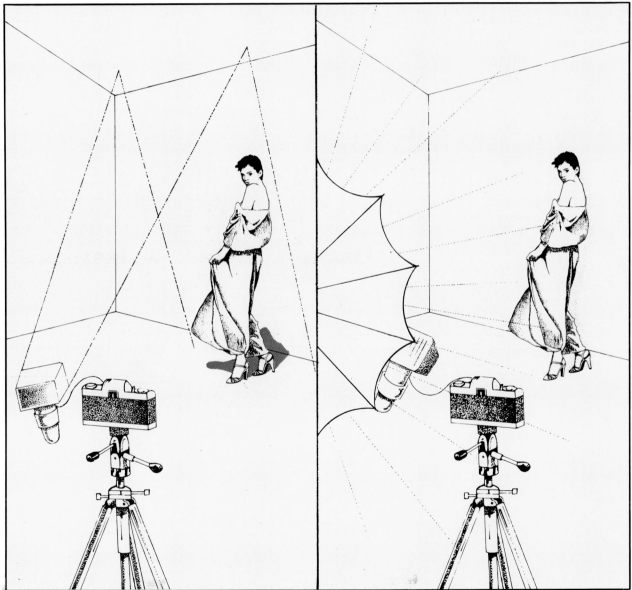

Top left and right: Direct flash results in a stark image of the model and an over-contrasted background. Use of a reflector softens the image and reveals form and texture.

Above left and right: Two good ways of diffusing the flashgun's light — either by reflecting from a white ceiling, creating soft top light, or from a white umbrella reflector.

Portraits and Artificial Lighting

To be able to photograph someone in an interesting way, sometimes dramatically, sometimes with flattery, is a sign of photographic achievement.

People may be photographed indoors or out, they may be isolated from their surroundings, or the environment may form an important part of the picture's construction; they may be pictured doing nothing or they may be busy with work or a hobby, they may look straight into the lens of the camera or away from it.

Outdoor Portraiture

People with simple cameras will find outdoor portraiture the most satisfactory. Location doesn't really matter all that much, unless you require model and surroundings to mould together into one artistic image. Disturbing, intruding backgrounds and foregrounds, however, should be avoided at all costs. Watch out for lamp posts and telegraph poles emerging from heads, railings which appear to go in one ear and out of the other, sharp horizons passing through the neck, garbage containers beside the model.

Most portraiture is best done with wide aperture settings, throwing both foreground and background out of focus. Trees and shrubs make better backdrops than buildings, even if they are well blurred, while some foreground color from a bed of flowers can work wonders.

The best portraits are shot with the sun behind the model. One drawback of this however, is that the face could be in too-deep shadow. If the picture is being taken on the beach, with plenty of light reflected up from light-colored sand, you may have no problems. Otherwise, as mentioned earlier, be prepared to reflect light into the face by having someone hold some form of reflector (an opened-up newspaper will do) in front of the subject, but out of shot.

Exposure metering in such cases must be precise; take care to meter for the model's face, not for the much brighter light coming from behind.

Indoor Portraiture

Many people consider that the most effective indoor portraits are those done completely without artificial light, the only light source being that which is naturally available in the room.

The best position for the model in such cases is beside a window. Sometimes the light might be strongly directional, illuminating only one side of the face. This could

There is no set of rules which enables you to guarantee success with portraits — the secret, usually, is to work out the situation with model, camera and lighting until it looks best through the viewfinder. An unusual stance was taken for this portrait, the girl keeping her back to the camera with her face turned round. However, it works well. Note how the use of a bright color in the girl's skirt brings the whole picture alive. A standard lens was used on a 35mm camera; the high speed film was exposed for 1/250 sec at f/8.

be a useful effect; but if you want more light on the shadow side, use a reflector.

With indoor portraiture, be prepared for exposures as long as one second if the light is rather low. Therefore a tripod is essential for the camera, which should be fired by cable release or by using the delay timer.

If you require an artificial light source you can always use table lamps, bedside lamps and household spot lamps. You may then wish to progress to authentic photographic lighting, which begins with simple spot and flood lamps.

Here's good use of window light, which has helped produce a superb photograph. The soft look can be achieved by smearing face cream around a clear filter fitted over the lens, leaving only the central area clear – an extremely effective (and very cheap) way of getting this type of result. Exposure would be 1/2 sec at f/5.6.

When using color reversal film with artificial lighting remember that the slides will have an overall orange-red cast unless you use a correction filter or buy film balanced for tungsten lighting. Color negative films do not need correction, because this is done at the printing stage.

Instant Pictures

Instant photography is fun and every household with any interest in photography should have an instant camera for those occasions when it is desirable to get a picture on the spot.

Even people using elaborate cameras find an instant camera a useful second-string, especially on vacation. Although the more advanced instant cameras can be used quite seriously, they do seem to encourage snapshooting and bring back the fun and simplicity which can evaporate as you become more serious about photography.

Instant film is at its best in bright sunlight – good reason for using it on the beach at vacation time. Usually, instant cameras are as simple to use as the simplest conventional type – aim, focus and press the button. When using one with automatic exposure control try to avoid taking pictures into the light, since if you do the auto system might expose for the background and not the main subject. One limitation of instant film is its requirement for accurate exposure control.

How Long Does it Take?

The newer types of instant camera use film which ejects from the camera after exposure and then develops itself in about eight to ten minutes. There's none of the peeling apart of the earlier systems.

However, peel-apart films are still very much in use. Follow the instructions carefully; if the development time is one minute, then allow exactly this time to elapse between pulling the sheet out of the camera and peeling off the outer covering, otherwise you may ruin the exposure.

Many companies will make duplicate prints from both Polaroid and Kodak instant prints, so that these systems are nearly as versatile as conventional negative-print systems.

Instant Flash

Instant film is just as well suited to flash photography as it is to sunny-weather use; in fact, some people consider the colors are even better when used with flash. Manufacturers realize that instant cameras have countless indoor uses, so they have gone to great trouble to ensure good quality in these conditions.

When using the specially designed flash bars, make sure you operate within the distance limitations. Get too close and the image will be over-exposed; too far away and it will be under-exposed.

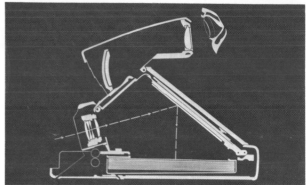

Light is reflected by a permanent mirror onto a Fresnel mirror, bundled into a beam and onto a third mirror. This reflects it through an aspheric eye piece, presenting the view in its true format. To take a picture, the Fresnel mirror folds up revealing a 'taking' mirror which reflects the light onto the negative.

The Polaroid SX-70 land camera combines several special facilities. It is a folding single lens reflex camera which produces instant pictures. Electronically controlled it automatically ejects the picture 1·5 seconds after the user releases the shutter. The picture then takes a short time to develop fully, but it is already dry and will complete its development even in very bright light.

Special Effects

Creativity in photography is not a mystique for the privileged few – in fact it begins when you first realize the differences between a straightforward snapshot and a well-thought-out picture.

No book could tell its readers how to take creative photographs, because that's not what creativity is all about. A photographer's creative limitations are bounded only by his own brain, and each creative picture is unique. However, there are certain techniques you can learn. For instance all photographers can use aperture and shutter speed, to make unusual effects to change a snapshot into a creative photograph.

Making things move

Deliberate blurring can be most effective. Even a simple shot such as someone walking along a street can be turned into a creative picture. Such a scene, photographed with a shutter speed of 1/8 sec or 1/4 sec would show a blurring of arms, legs, and background. The same applies to any other moving subject.

It is of course important to understand which techniques will create which type of result if you are going to get the results you want. If you are photographing a moving subject and want to get a contrast between it and a still background, then a slow shutter speed will achieve your aim. The slower the shutter speed the more the subject will be blurred and the greater the contrast will be. If you pan the camera in the direction of the subject's movement, again using a slow shutter speed, the background will be more blurred than the subject, giving a highly effective impression of speed.

Even perfectly static subjects can be given movement. One way is to move the camera during exposure; using a speed of 1/2 sec to photograph a tree, deliberately moving the camera, could give an idea of a storm, with the tree being blown around in the wind.

Another way is to use a zoom lens, deliberately altering the zoom setting during exposure. You'll need a speed of 1/2 sec or even a full second, moving the zoom from one end of its range to the other while the shutter is open. The effects can be quite startling.

You can also use a slow shutter speed to emphasize the stillness of one object in contrast to a moving background.

Trick Photography

While some unusual things may be done with fairly simple cameras, photographers possessing single lens reflex models are alone in being limited solely by their own ideas. Whatever kind of effect one wishes to achieve, there is usually some way of doing it.

Blurring to suggest movement has been mentioned already. But there are other occasions when a blurred image can tell a story.

Rotating the camera during a long exposure is one idea which works particularly well at night. The camera may be hand-held for this, or rotated more scientifically on a tripod (provided it has a suitable head).

Special effects in color are not only for the professional; any amateur photographer with a little patience and a reasonable camera can achieve quite unusual results. One useful trick is to make sandwiches of two or three separate images all put together in one transparency holder. They can then either be projected for viewing, or rephotographed to form a final, all-in-one image. Both the picture of the cooling tower with trees, and the one on the next page of the people walking in front of a large image of the sun, are examples of this technique. Experiment is the key to success here; the only real rule worth remembering is to slightly over-expose each image so that the final result is not too dark.

Multiple Images

A great variety of special effects may be achieved with multiple images. With this technique, the impossible may be made to happen with the camera – such as people walking on water or the tops of buildings, upside-down trees, ships sailing down the Main Street and so on.

In order to prevent accidental multiple images, camera designers these days always incorporate prevention devices. Some cameras have special multiple exposure controls to permit the deliberate use of this appealing effect. If yours does not, a multiple exposure can be made by depressing the film rewind button (which is usually in the base of the camera) at the same time as the film wind-on lever is activated. The rewind button, when depressed, ensures that the film is not wound on, while the wind-on lever re-sets the shutter. This may be repeated as many times as required.

The viewfinder must be used with extreme care when making a double exposure in order to achieve the desired effect. For example, it would be no good having an image purporting to show a tree growing out of the deck of a ship if the two exposures had not been correctly aligned and the tree was floating over the ship.

Multiple images may also be achieved by sandwiching two transparencies in one mount, or by printing more than one negative on the same sheet of paper.

Using techniques like these you can combine natural subjects with abstract patterns in an artistic way.

Projectors and Reflectors

Projectors may also be used for special effects. You can photograph someone standing in front of a projected image and, with the correct lighting balance, produce a very realistic image. Another use of projectors is to throw an image, often an abstract one, onto a person's body, or any other light colored object.

Mirrors, lenses and pieces of colored paper can all be used to produce something different. All good photographic dealers stock multi-image lenses and other devices for a wide range of effects.

Some of the most successful indoor pictures of girls are like this one, where the only light is that coming through the window. You can use a filter to give a slightly soft appearance to the picture, and drastically up-rate the film to give the moody, grainy appearance. With the camera tripod mounted you could use a 200 ASA reversal film at 1600 ASA, exposing and processing accordingly, to achieve this type of result.

This third photograph is the result of a carefully planned and well-executed multiple-exposure technique. A series of exposures have been taken without advancing the film, to give the impression that the subject is moving across the picture. Again, practice is the only road to success.

Close Ups and Delayed Exposure

Close-ups are possible with most cameras, but only with an SLR can you move into the true area of macrophotography.

Getting a Close-up Lens

Close-up lenses may be purchased for use with simple, pocket cameras, permitting more detailed pictures of a range of subjects. But only with SLR models can the effect of close-up attachments be seen through the viewfinder. With all other cameras, close-up lenses must be used at a fixed camera-to-subject distance, and the camera lined up to the subject by a combination of guesswork and measurement.

Close-ups can also be taken by fitting any magnifying glass over the camera lens, then focusing and exposing normally. Quite dramatic enlargements can be achieved, with surprisingly good quality.

Specialist close-up equipment starts with close-up lenses which screw into the camera's filter mount. These lenses are not expensive, and may be bought in varying strengths.

Using Extension Tubes

Another inexpensive method is to use extension tubes which are fitted between the camera and lens; the resultant extension provides image magnification. If meter-coupled tubes are required (to permit full use of the camera's TTL metering) they do become more expensive, particularly if your camera possesses one of the more complex coupling systems. They are available in three sizes (1, 2 and 3) and may be used individually or in combination.

To get maximum lens extension you will need extension bellows units, which provide variable lens-to-camera distances. These may be used with extension tubes and with a variety of lenses.

Extending the camera-to-lens distance necessitates an exposure increase. If the extension device permits use of the camera's built-in metering system, then exposure metering is done exactly as usual, with no need to allow for an increase. If not, you will have to refer to exposure increase tables, which are often supplied with close-up equipment.

Other close-up methods include reversing rings for the lens (which provides magnification).

Maximizing the Depth of Field

One serious drawback to close-up photography is that the depth-of-field decreases with increases in magnification. With a bellows unit used at maximum extension, depth of field will be only a few millimeters at average apertures, so always reckon on using the smallest possible aperture setting, unless you aim to produce pictures with only a minute area of sharpness.

Delayed Exposures

Most cameras are fitted with a delay timer which, on maximum setting, gives an average of 10 seconds delay from the time it is activated to the moment of shutter release. By using this device the photographer can appear in the picture himself.

To use the delay timer, place the camera on a tripod or a firm support. The picture should be pre-composed, taking care to allow for the extra figure, and the exposure controls set. After operating the delay control, all you have to do is to move into position.

A delay timer can also be used to prevent camera shake when using slow shutter speeds. It is useful for both hand-held or tripod-mounted situations, since even when using a tripod, depressing the release in the usual way can cause some movement.

Spiders' webs make fascinating nature studies, whether photographed in full with a standard lens (as here) or in minute detail with macro equipment. One important thing to remember is to have the light shining through the web, showing up its fascinating near-luminous qualities. The best time of year for pictures like this is September and October, early in the morning.

Although this is not a true close-up, it is probably as near as many people will want to venture into this fascinating world. Not many cameras will permit sufficiently close focusing to produce a satisfactory image of a flower. The answer, as was done here, is to fit a close-up lens over the primary lens. Because, with close-ups, depth of field becomes extremely limited, aim to use the smallest aperture possible, and always mount the camera on a tripod. Exposure for this shot would be 1/15 sec at f/11 on slow-speed film.

The Professionals

There is no reason why anyone interested in photography should allow his involvement in the subject to stop short at showing pictures to family and friends. A whole world awaits the keen photographer, such as photo competitions, press work and photo libraries. Also, there's the intense enjoyment that can come from joining a photographic club.

Winning Competitions

Competitions are an enormous potential source of income. In any one year photographic magazines promote competitions worth thousands of dollars. Additionally, there are promotional competitions put on by commercial organizations who regard photographic involvement as a way of stimulating interest in their products or services.

This photograph won a competition for a vacation company who were looking for shots showing the peace and tranquility of Norway. Its winning qualities are a combination of good composition, right camera angle and good use of available color.

Any good photographer should be able to win at least one contest in a year. There are a number of highly proficient amateur photographers who specialize in entering contests and who have, over the years, scooped up some extremely valuable prizes.

Anyone contemplating entering a competition should study its rules and general conditions. You should be able to ascertain the type of photographs being looked for, and then plan accordingly.

Press Photography

Press work can be lucrative for the amateur working on a freelance basis. The key qualities are specialization, opportunism, quality and downright perseverance.

One good introduction to press work is through the local newspapers who often print off-beat pictures, sometimes in their own right and sometimes with feature articles. Startling news pictures, also, sell to newspapers.

Specialist journalism, however, is likely to be more rewarding. Choose a subject, or range of subjects, about which you have some knowledge, and which are well covered in magazines and newspapers. Submit material of good quality and which is well presented.

Libraries and Agencies

Many photographers choose to sell their work through photographic libraries or agencies. But there is no point in attempting this unless you are capable of producing excellent photographs in transparency format.

Newspapers, magazines, commercial companies and publicity organizations have agency contacts who they get in touch with when they want pictures. Agencies

Photographs like this are often used for advertising; this one would be ideal for agricultural products or for certain foods, such as breakfast cereals. Pictures of this type and quality are usually shot by professionals, but there's no reason why the competent amateur, with good equipment, should not come up to this standard. If you do, going to a good photographic agency is the most likely way to get it sold, although a direct approach to an advertising agency can sometimes work.

To get pictures of lightning the photographer must have extreme patience, and be prepared to go out into the open in the middle of a raging storm. The only way is to wait until the lightning starts and then, with the camera on a tripod, leave the shutter open for as long as you like (up to several minutes if you feel like it). During that time, each flash of lightning will leave its trace on the film. Attempts to photograph individual lightning flashes, with brief shutter speeds, will almost always fail.

can usually help you because they have extensive files.

The two chief drawbacks are that your slides could remain on their files for years, and the agency will charge a high commission (around 50%) for selling your work.

Photographic Clubs

There's no financial gain from belonging to a photographic club, but they do engender a spirit of competition, and this is the most direct route to improvement. Joining a club, and entering wholeheartedly into its activities could well teach you more about photography in a year than could be otherwise grasped in five years. With photo clubs, enthusiasts get the chance to do forms of photography that would not otherwise come their way.

Addresses of local camera clubs can be obtained from most libraries and local information offices.

Home Processing and Printing

The magic of photography is not complete without some experience of home processing and printing. The best way to start off is to develop black and white films, and make prints from your own negatives. There is nothing difficult about home processing and it will make your hobby much more interesting.

Processing

Essential requirements are:

> Developing tank; accurate thermometer; measuring flasks (one large, one small); developer; fixer.

Optional extras include:

> Light-tight changing bag (for loading the developing tank); extra flasks; pouring funnel; photographic timer; squeegee film wiper; photographic wetting agent; force film washer.

To process the film; follow this procedure:

1. In total darkness load the film into the developing tank spirals and fit the lid securely (a).

2. Pre-warm the developing tank to around 20°C (if the weather is cold) by leaving in a warm room.

3. Mix the developer with water, strictly to makers' instructions, ensuring that the diluted developer is at the recommended temperature (usually 20°C). Check you have the correct amount of developer.

4. Pour the developer into the tank (b), noting the time carefully. Immediately agitate for a full 20 seconds or repeatedly invert the tank several times.

5. Agitate or invert every 60 seconds (c).

6. Check the temperature during development by inserting thermometer into tank (unnecessary if room is at developing temperature).

7. Remove tank top and commence pouring out developer a few seconds before stipulated time, so that tank is emptied on time (d).

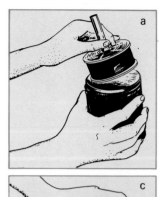
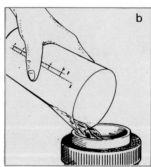

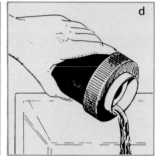

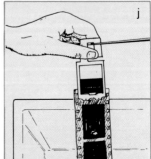

8. Pour in a water rinse or stop bath rinse at 20°C (e).

9. Remove rinse (f) and pour in fixer (g), which should be at roughly the same temperature.

10. Pour out fixer (it is re-usable, remember) after stipulated time (h). Do not leave fixer in too long, otherwise bleaching could result.

11. Check that film is perfectly cleared. If it looks milky at this stage it is not properly fixed.

12. Wash with running water or, preferably, a force washer, for at least 25 minutes (i).

13. Add a few drops of wetting agent after turning off the wash, to break surface tension.

14. Remove film from spiral, wiping off excess water.

15. Hang to dry in a clean area, weighting the bottom to prevent curling (j).

16. Cut the film into suitable lengths for inserting into storage bags or sleeves.

Making prints

Making black and white prints is no more difficult than processing a film. However, print quality can be affected by a number of controllable variables, so great care should be taken at every stage. Print making does not require a specialist darkroom, and can be done perfectly satisfactorily in a blacked-out bathroom or kitchen – the latter being preferable because of the accessibility of power points.

Essential requirements for printmaking are:

Enlarger; accurate thermometer; clock with sweep seconds hand or darkroom timer; three print dishes; paper; developer; fixer; safelight.

Optional extras include:

Sensor/timer for easier exposure assessment; print washer; print drier.

To make a print follow this procedure:

1. Place the negative in the enlarger which should be adjusted for the right column height to provide the required degree of enlargement. The enlarger aperture should be set, ideally fairly small to provide optimum image sharpness, although this will mean slightly longer exposures. Focus it with care.

2. Find the required exposure either by using a sensor/timer or a test strip (a strip of paper is exposed in strips of varying exposure and then developed to show the optimum exposure).

3. Place a sheet of paper on the masking frame or baseboard and expose for the determined time.

4. Slide paper into developer tray (which should be at 20°C), sliding in and out for even development, without air bubbles, for the full development time recommended by the developer manufacturer.

5. Remove paper from developer to rinse/stop bath (water is quite adequate).

6. Place paper in fixer for stipulated time.

7. Wash print in running water for at least 25 minutes.

8. Hang print to dry (if resin coated type) or glaze if glossy type.

developer   stop bath   fixer   rinse/dry

Index

Published by Chartwell Books Inc., A Division of Book Sales Inc., 110 Enterprise Avenue, Secaucus, New Jersey 07094. ISBN 0-89009-288-5. L of C No. 79-52930.